How to Make a Simple and Comprehensive Action Research: A Guide

Zacky Zacarias L. Cadorna II
Stephen C. Baldado
Marissa B. Cadorna

© 2015
ISBN: 978-1512037548

How to Make a Simple and Comprehensive Action research:
A Guide

Printed in the United States of America

First Printing, 2015

Createspace
7290 Investment Drive Suite B
North Charleston, SC 29418
USA

ISBN: 978-1512037548

The authors would like to express their heartfelt gratitude to the supervisor of Manjuyod District 2, Dr. Dominador E. Bersa and the District Supervisor of Ayungon, Mrs. Leonivel L. Secusana for their supports in the publication and reproduction of this book.

Z. Z. L. Cadorna II

S. C. Baldado

M. B. Cadorna

TABLE OF CONTENTS

Page

Preface 5
What is Action Research? 6
Why should teachers conduct action research? 6
How Action Research differs from basic researches? 6
ACTION RESEARCH FORMAT 7
WHAT TO WRITE IN EACH PART?
TITLE 9
PROBLEM 11
Action Research Question 11
Research Hypothesis 12
Action Plan 13
Collection, Presentation and Interpretation of Data 16
Results and Recommendations 19
References 21
APPENDICES
Appendix A
THE ACTION RESEARCH OUTLINE 22
Appendix B
Sample Action Plan 26
Appendix C
SAMPLE COVER PAGE 27

Appendix D
SAMPLE APPROVAL SHEET 28

Appendix E
Action Research Flow Chart 29

Appendix F

Ready-Made Action Research 30

PREFACE

The writers of this manual intended to provide guidance to all teachers, School Heads, and writers of Action Research papers. Its format and samples of how each part should be presented provide basic information that can be easily understood, for it is designed to present a simple yet comprehensive way to conduct studies in at least classroom settings.

The outline and text format of the report, sample approval sheet, sample action plan, and the procedures of conducting school action research in the Department of Education are all presented in the appendices to provide concrete information, and optimum guidance to the writers. Though specifically designed for DepEd Teachers of Manjuyod District II and Ayungon District in the Division of Negros Oriental, Philippines, it may serve other schools from other Districts, Divisions, Department, as well.

Z.L.C.II.
S.C.B.
M.B.C

What is Action Research?

There are many definitions of Action Research written by different authors. The following are some of the culled definitions from internet and books.

- Any action undertaken by teachers to collect data and evaluate their own teaching (Brown & Robinsons).
- An interactive method of collecting information that is used to explore topics of teaching, curriculum development and student behavior in the classroom (education-portal.com).
- is either research initiated to solve an immediate problem or a reflective process of progressive problem solving led by individuals working with others in teams or as part of a "community of practice" to improve the way they address issues and solve problems (wikipedia.org).

Why should teachers conduct Action Research?

As teachers, they need to know:
1. What is actually happening in the classroom?
2. What learners are thinking?
3. Why learners are reacting in the ways they do?
4. What aspects in our classroom we should focus on.

How Action Research differs from basic researches?

Difference Between Basic Research and Action Research		
Criteria	Basic Research	Action Research
Objectives	Develop and test educational theory and derive generalizations.	To find solutions to problems in a specific context.
Trainings	Intensive training is needed in Research Methodology.	Limited training is needed.
Selection of a problem	A wide range of methods are used to select a problem.	Participating teacher identify problems during

		the teaching-learning processes.
Hypothesis	Highly specific hypotheses are developed.	Specific statement of the problem serves as hypotheses.
Conclusions	Conclusions may be in the form of generalizations and developing theories.	Findings are local/specific.
Applications or results	The generalizations have broad applicability.	Findings are used immediately in the classroom situations by participating teachers to improve their own practices.

Furthermore, Action Research is not really a tedious task that most of the novice researchers thought, for they believed that its procedures and sequence in the conduct of the study is like conducting thesis writing. Action Research can be done from 2 to 3 pages only.

ACTION RESEARCH FORMAT

There's a lot of Action Research Format that can be taken from the internet. Due to this, many novice researchers and teachers were confused which of which is to be followed, and most reliable. The truth is no matter how it is presented as long as the conduct of the study is systematic, and accepted by the authorities of the Department where the study was conducted it is reliable. However, it would be better if the Action Research Paper is written in the simplest way.

The following format is the result of a thorough discussion between the School Head Mr. Lemuel B. Anfone and the researcher Mr. Zacky Zacarias L. Cadorna II, when Mr. Cadorna conducted and wrote his first   action research in Manjuyod National High School. Due to the brief and comprehensive presentations of each part, it has been adopted by other researchers not only in Manjuyod National High School but also in other schools, as well.

❖ **TITLE**

o **Object of the Study**
o **Sample Population**
o **Setting or Research Site**

❖ **PROBLEM**
o **Statement of the Problem**
o **Suggested Intervention**
o **Anchored Theories (If there's any)**

❖ **ACTION RESEARCH QUESTION(S)**

❖ **RESEARCH HYPOTHESIS**
o **Null hypothesis (Ho)**
o **Alternative Hypothesis (Ha)**

❖ **ACTION PLAN**

❖ **COLLECTION, PRESENTATION, AND INTERPRETATION OF DATA**

o **Statistical Tool**
o **Table**
o **Interpretation**

❖ **RESULTS**

o **Conclusion**

RECOMMENDATION(S)

WHAT TO WRITE IN EACH PART?

Most of the Heads especially in the Department of Education are too busy with their paper works, reports, and other job related and personal tasks. Thus, when you present your Action Research report it must be direct to the point, specific and the sequence must be congruent with each other from title to recommendations.

To present the simple ways on how and what to write in each of the part of the action research, the authors just simply provided samples of each segment that can guide the action research writers especially the beginners in writing their studies.

TITLE

In the other types of research, the title is usually presented in a question form. But, in action research, the title focuses directly on the effectiveness, relevance, impact (and the likes) of the intervention (solution) to treat the problem.

It is usually constructed in three parts:

First is the object of the study, **Second** is the sample population, and **Third** is the setting or research site.

The following pictures were taken in the actual documentations of the Action Research conducted by Mr. S. Baldado of Manjuyod National High School in the Division of Negros Oriental. Try to look into them, and construct an appropriate title by answering the following questions.

Manjuyod National High School

Flag Raising Ceremony						
Attendance Sheet						
Date:_____						
Section: GYPSUM-VII SY 2014 - 2015						

Name of Students	FEBRUARY					TOTAL
	2	3	4	5	5	
1.Aboyabor,kevin,Palumar	1	0	0	0	0	1
2.Abrasado,Franz,Jzyrell,Andaya	0	0	0	0	0	0
3.Abrasaldo,Gally Jr.,Cadalin	0	0	0	0	0	0
4.Abueva,Ever Coderu	1	0	0	0	1	2
5.Acabal,Jestone,Alabata	0	0	1	1	0	2

Activity 1:

Based on the pictures presented above;

1. What would be the object of the study?
   Object of the study: _____

2. Who were the respondents?
   Sample population: _____

3. Where was the study conducted?
   Setting (research site): _____

Indeed, it is very easy to answer the questions above if you just follow the ideas in writing the Action Research Tittle that were mentioned earlier. So, answering the three basic questions are really the simple steps in guiding the researcher in writing his Action Research Tittle. To elaborate, the example below is presented as vivid appearance on how Action Research Tittle must be presented based on the above given situation as shown in the pictures.

"The Impact of Classroom Adviser's Presence in Improving the Grade VII – Gypsum Students' Attendance during Flag Raising Ceremony in Manjuyod National High School in the School Year 2014 - 2015"

(1) Object of the study: The Impact of Classroom Adviser's Presence in Improving Students' Attendance during Flag Ceremony.

(2) Sample population: Grade VII – Gypsum Students in the School Year 2014 – 2015

(3) Setting (research site): Manjuyod National High School

PROBLEM

Problem is the core of the study. Finding or formulating what to write in the problem stage is really a problem to most novice researchers. However, there are simple ways in formulating it.

TWO SIMPLE WAYS TO WRITE IN THE PART OF THE PROBLEM

Formulating what to write in the Problem Part of the study is as simple as the following:

First – State the problem

Example: **Students' Attendance during Flag Ceremony** is one of the most critical problems of the advisers...

Second – State the intervention which you believe that can treat or minimize the problem.

Example: In line with the aforesaid problem, the researcher of this study tries to investigate if **the presence of Classroom adviser** has an impact in improving students' attendance during flag ceremony.

o Anchored theories, Republic Act and Memorandum (If there's any)

Linking or anchoring the study to any existing Theory, Republic Act, and Memorandum is optional. However, it is very important to make your research more accurate and reliable.

Example: This scenario links to Albert Bandura's Observational Learning Theory, in which he postulated that we can learn by observing others. He claimed that modeling can have as much impact as direct experience.

Activity 2

Before proceeding to the next segment in Action Research writing, try to answer the following questions, for these will guide you in writing your study.

1. What is a very common problem that you have encountered in school (Students, teachers, etc.)?
2. Think of an intervention that you believe that could treat or minimize the problem.
3. Construct an Appropriate Title out of the problem and intervention you have identified.
4. Then, formulate a rationale in line with your constructed Action Research Title under the "Problem" part.

Action Research Question

What is an Action Research Question?

An Action Research question guides your study. It should focus on the planned intervention to be used in the research. Unlike other basic researches, the questions in Action Research are just stated in the simplest way that could be answerable by yes or no.

Example: Does **Classroom adviser's presence** have an impact in improving students' attendance during the school's daily flag raising ceremony?

The above example focuses directly on the **planned intervention** of the study, the **Classroom adviser's presence.**

Research Hypothesis

It is the researcher's assumption about the intervention she/he has introduced. This is her/his perception that answers her/his formulated research question. It could be stated in positive or negative way (Null Hypothesis).

Negative (Null Hypothesis)
Example:

H_o

Classroom Adviser's presence has no impact in improving students' attendance during the school's daily flag raising ceremony.

Positive (Alternative hypothesis)
Example:

Ha

Classroom Adviser's presence has an impact in improving students' attendance during the school's daily flag raising ceremony. (Positive)

The researcher must choose only one hypothesis either positive or negative. It is also important to use the symbols (H_o or Ha). Use H_o if Negative and H_a if Positive.

Activity 3

In activity 2, you have already formulated your Action Research Title, and constructed the rationale of your study under the Problem Part. Now, out of it write your Action Research question and Action Research Hypothesis.

Action Research Question: _____

Action Research Hypothesis: _____

Action Plan

In **School Action Research**, this part is a systematic presentation of events <u>before,</u> <u>during,</u> and <u>after</u> the conduct of the planned intervention. Most of the Action Plans are directly presented in tabular forms, but in Action Research the sequential conduct of the study must be stated first before presenting the table that displays the whole picture of the proceedings being conducted.

Example:

To able to answer the research question, the researcher of this study planned and conducted the actions below:

1. Submission of Pertinent documents for approval

2. After the approval of the Schools Division Superintendent , the researcher immediately conducted the following interventions to investigate the impact the classroom advisers' presence in improving students' attendance during flag raising ceremony in the two situations:

2.1 February 23-27, 2015. The researcher attended the flag raising ceremony far enough to be seen by his advisory class while keeps tracking his advisory class attendance through his designated checker for one week.
2.2 March 2-6, 2015. The researcher attended the flag raising ceremony in front of his advisory class on March 2-6, 2015 and will track his advisory class attendance in one week.

3. The researcher collected the data on students' attendance for one week without the adviser's presence in front of the line during a flag raising ceremony and one week after the intervention.

4.....

ACTIVITIES	TIME FRAME	RESOURCES NEEDED	Persons Involved	Success Indicator/ Remarks
1.1 Submission of the letter of intent and research proposal to the Principal	February 2,2015	Bondpaper	Principal Researcher/s	Completed
1.2 Submission of the Endorsement	February 3, 2015	Bondpaper, Folder	Principal, District Supervisor, Researcher/s	Completed

letter from the Principal to the District Supervisor				
1.3 Submission of Endorsement letter from the District Supervisor to the Schools Division Superintendent for the approval of the research	February 10,2015	Bondpaper, Folder	Schools Division Superintendent Principal, Researcher/s	Completed
2. Conduct of the study.	February 23 – March 6, 2015	Attendance sheet (Data gathering tool), folder	Students (respondents) , Researcher	To be Accomplished
3....	....	....	...	

Note: The Action Plan must be written in future tenses in the Action Research proposal.

Activity 4

In activity 2 and 3, you have crafted already your Action Research Title, Problem, Questions, and Hypothesis. Now, construct a systematic Action Plan of the conduct of your study.

Just follow the procedures presented above.

----

1. _____

_____

2. _____

_____

ACTIVITIES	TIME FRAME	RESOURCES NEEDED	Persons Involved	Success Indicator/ Remarks

Collection, Presentation and Interpretation of Data

In this part, the researcher must state how he gathered the data. The presentation of data must be tabulated and be interpreted briefly based on the findings.

Most of the researchers used "high – statistical tools" in interpreting the data, but in Action Research, it is not necessary. According to Mr. Lemuel B. Anfone, the principal of Manjuyod National High School, Division of Negros Oriental, "Why use such statistical tools if the results are already evident in the presented data"? Mean Percentage Score (MPS), Simple Percentage, Scaling, Ranking System, Mean, Median, Mode and the Likes are advised to use for measuring the data.

Example:
The data presented on the tables below was taken during the School's Flag Raising Ceremony.

TABLE 1: Pre – Intervention Week
Students' Flag Ceremony Attendance
N = 50

DAY	ATTENDANCE	% of Participation
1	7	14%
2	18	36%
3	20	40%
4	22	44%
5	21	42%
TOTAL AVERAGE	17.6	35.2%

Based on Table No. 1, the total average of 7 Gypsum students who attended in the flag raising ceremony during the pre-intervention week is only 17.6 or 35.2% out of 50 students.

TABLE 2: Intervention Week
Students' Flag Ceremony Attendance
N = 50

DAY	ATTENDANCE	% of Participation
1	9	18%
2	25	50%
3	35	70%
4	44	88%
5	39	78%
TOTAL AVERAGE	30.4	60.8%

Based on Table No. 2, the total average of Gypsum 7 students who attended the flag raising ceremony during the intervention is 30.4 or 60.8 % out of 50 students.

Look, the interpretations above are just simply restating the data being presented on the tables in words. The researcher used only a simple percentage in interpreting the data.

Note: Table presentations depend on the conducted study.

What statistical tool to be used?

Once again, please be reminded by the following in writing the part of "Collection, Presentation and Interpretation of Data" in your Action Research.

o The Researcher may not use higher statistical instrument. According to Mr. Lemuel B. Anfone, the School Head of Manjuyod National High School, and Research Specialist, "Why use such statistical tools if the results are already evident in the presented data."

o Mean Percentage Score (MPS), Simple Percentage, Scaling, Ranking System, Mean, Median, Mode and the Likes are advised to use for measuring the data.

Data Gathering Tool

The most common type of Data Gathering Instrument being used in other researches like in thesis writing and dissertations are in the form of questionnaires, wherein the respondents shall only check on the box that corresponds to their answers to the formative questions.

In Action Research, Attendance Sheets, Class Records, Tally Sheets and the likes can be used as Data Gathering Instrument. Look at the following samples.

Sample 1:

This can be used in gathering data during Flag Raising Ceremony.

Manjuyod National High School
Daily Flag Raising Ceremony Attendance Sheet
Grade 7 Gypsum
SY 2014 – 2015

Name of Students	Date					TOTAL
	3/2/2015	3/3/2015	3/4/2015	3/5/2015	3/6/2015	
	Signature	Signature	Signature	Signature	Signature	
1. Bradly, Timothy						
2. Mayweather, Timothy						
3. Morales, Erik						
4. Pacqiao, Manny						

Prepared by:

_____
Adviser

Noted by:
_____
Principal

Sample 2:

Data gathering instrument for Mean Percentage Scores Tracking in Formative Exams

Grade 7 Gypsum
English Formative Tests Scores

Name of Students	FORMATIVE TEST SCORES									TOTAL
	3/2/2015	SIGNATURE	3/3/2015		3/4/2015		3/5/2015		3/6/2015	
1. Bradly, Timothy										
2. Mayweather, Timothy										
3. Morales, Erik										
4. Pacqiao, Manny										
Number of Items										
Number of Takers										
Mean Score										
MPS										

Prepared by:

Adviser

Noted by:

Principal

Activity 5

1. Design a data gathering tool, and fill it out with your imaginary data.
2. Construct tables with necessary information based on the data you have provided.
3. Be sure that the data is congruent to the ideas you have made in the previous activities.

Results

This part is the answer of Action Research question, or the conclusion of the researcher based on the findings of the study.

Example:

Based on the findings of this study, Classroom Adviser's presence has an impact in improving students' attendance during schools daily Flag Raising Ceremony.

Note: The researcher can only conclude that the intervention has an impact/effect in **improving something, or in minimizing a problem** if the finding during the intervention period is **at least 5 % higher or lower** than the result during pre – intervention period **(Ojario, 2015).** Therefore, if the results during intervention period are higher in at least 5% than the pre – intervention week, the researcher may conclude that the intervention given has an impact in improving of minimizing something.

Recommendations

In this part, the researcher must state his/her suggestions or further actions based on the results or conclusion in the study.

Example:

In light with the findings of this study, the following recommendations are presented below:

1. The classroom Adviser should be in front of the line of his advisory class during the school's daily flag raising ceremony in order to maintain a regular attendance of his advisory class.

2. It is also recommended that the school administrator/s should impose mandatory actions that will direct all classroom advisers and non-adviser teachers to regularly attend the school's daily flag raising ceremony.

Note: if the findings show that the intervention is not effective in treating or minimizing the problem, the researcher should suggest other mediation. Thus, that would be another action research.

References

Nugent, G., Malik, S., & Hollingsworth, S. (2012). A Practical Guide to Action Research for Literacy Educators: Global Operations Unit, International Reading Association, 444 N. Capitol St., Suite 640, Washington, DC 2001, USA.

McLeod, S. A. (2011). Bandura - Social Learning Theory. Retrieved May 5, 2015 from http://www.simplypsychology.org/bandura.html

Sojor, H., Sitoy, T.V, Olis, B. (2004). THESIS/DISSERTATION WRITING: A GUIDE: Graduate School, NEGROS ORIENTAL STATE UNIVERSITY, Dumaguete City

http://educ.queensu.ca/projects/action_research/15quote.htm

Sabando, M.M, (2015). Systematic Action Planning

BALDADO, S. (2015). The Impact of Classroom Adviser's Presence in Improving the Grade VII – Gypsum Students' Attendance during Flag Raising Ceremony in Manjuyod National High School in the School Year 2014 – 2015: An Action Research

CADORNA, Z.L, (2015). The Effects of Multi-balls Feeding in Enhancing the Backhand – Topspin Stroke of the Table Tennis Players in Manjuyod National High School in the School Year 2014 – 2015: An Action Research

MEDEZ, A., (2015). Action Research: Retrieved March 2, 2015 from manjuyodsciencehigh.weebly.com

APPENDICES

Appendix A

Action Research Outline

Title

- It is usually constructed in three parts:
- First is the object of the study
- Second is the sample population, and
- Third is the setting or research site.

By:

Problem

- First – State the problem
- Second – State the intervention which you believe that can treat or minimize the problem.

Action Research Question

- Research question should focus on the planned intervention in the study.

------------------------------------?

Research Hypothesis

- It is the researcher's assumption about the intervention she/he has introduced.
- This is her/his perception that answers her/his formulated research question.
- It could be stated in positive or negative way (Null Hypothesis).

Negative (Null Hypothesis)

H_o

Positive (Alternative hypothesis)

Ha

Action Plan

- This part is a systematic presentation of the events before, during, and after the conduct of the planned intervention.

To be able to answer the research question, the researcher of this study will undertake the following actions below:

1. _____
_____

2. _____
_____

3. _____
_____

4. _____
_____

Activities	Time Frame	Resources Needed	Persons Involved	Remarks/Success Indicators
1.				
2.				
3.				
4.				

Collection, Presentation and Interpretation of Data
- The researcher must state how he gathered the data.
- The presentation of data must be tabulated.
- Then, shall be interpreted comprehensively why such findings go that way.

Table 1
Ex. Pre – Test

Table 2
Ex. Post – Test

Note: Table presentation depends on the study conducted.

Results

- This part is the answer of Action Research question, or the conclusion of the researcher based on the findings of the study.

    Based on the findings presented on the table above, ------------------
    ----

Recommendation

- In this part, the researcher must state his/her suggestions or further actions based on the results or conclusion in the study.

    In light with the findings of this study, the following recommendations are presented below:

1.
2.
3.
4.

Appendix B

Sample Action Plan

ACTIVITIES	TIME FRAME	RESOURCES NEEDED	Persons Involved	Success Indicator/ Remarks
1.1 Submission of the letter of intent and research proposal to the Principal.	February 2,2015	Bondpaper	Principal Researcher/s	**Completed**
1.2 Submission of the Endorsement letter from the Principal to the District Supervisor.	February 3, 2015	Bondpaper, Folder	Principal, District Supervisor, Researcher/s	**Completed**
1.3 Submission of Endorsement letter from the District Supervisor to the Schools Division Superintendent for the approval of the research.	February 10,2015	Bondpaper, Folder	Schools Division Superintendent, Principal, Researcher/s	
2..............	....	....	.....	...

Appendix C

SAMPLE COVER PAGE

The Effects of Multi-balls Feeding in Enhancing the Backhand Topspin
Stroke
of the Table Tennis Players in Manjuyod National High School
in the School Year 2014 - 2015:

An Action Research
Presented to

MANJUYOD NATIONAL HIGH SCHOOL FACULTY

By:

ZACKY ZACARIAS L. CADORNA II
SST – III, MAPEH
Manjuyod NHS

Appendix D

**SAMPLE
APPROVAL SHEET**

-

This Action Research entitled "The Effects of Multi-balls Feeding in Enhancing the Backhand – Topspin Stroke of the Table Tennis Players in Manjuyod National High School in the School Year 2014 - 2015" prepared and submitted by ZACKY ZACARIAS L. CADORNA II has been reviewed and approved by the following:

LUZALIM L. ABUSO   HELBERT P. OJARIO
English Critic   Statistician, Manjuyod NHS
SST – I, Manjuyod NHS   Teacher III, Mathematics

LEMUEL B. ANFONE
Principal – I
Manjuyod National High School

DOMINADOR E. BERSA, Ed. D.   ALLAN A. TABIO
PSDS   EPS – I, MAPEH
Manjuyod District II   PESS Coordinator
         Division of Negros Oriental

SALUSTIANO T. JIMENEZ, Ll.B., CESO VI
Schools Division Superintendent

Note: The approval sheet must be placed/attached right after the cover page of the Action Research.

"Procedures of Conducting School Action Research"

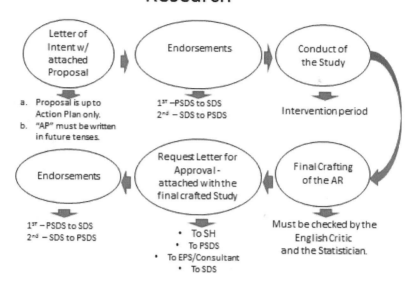

Note: Each School has its own procedure in the conduct of the study. The procedure of conducting Action Research presented above is based on the DepEd – Division of Negros Oriental, Philippines.

The Effects of Multi-balls Feeding in Enhancing the Backhand Topspin Stroke of the Table Tennis Players in Manjuyod National High School in the School Year 2014 - 2015: An Action Research

By:

Zacky Zacarias L. Cadorna II
TEACHER 3, MAPEH

Problem

Most of the athletes in the racket games like Table Tennis have difficulty in receiving or returning balls using the Back-Hand Topspin Stroke. This problem was proved by the researcher of this study when he conducted a 20 – balls feeding PRE – TEST for his players' accuracy in returning balls using forehand and backhand topspin strokes.

Due to the aforesaid problem, the table tennis coach, the researcher of this study, thought that Multi-Balls Feeding Strategy is effective in enhancing the Backhand – Topspin Stroke of his athletes. Thus, he tried to probe if the aforesaid strategy is really effective in improving his athletes' skills in receiving or returning balls using the Backhand – Topspin Stroke.

Action Research Question

Is Multi – balls Feeding effective in enhancing the Backhand - Topspin Stroke of the Table Tennis Players?

Research Hypothesis

Multi – balls Feeding is not effective in enhancing the Backhand – Topspin Stroke of the Table Tennis Players.

Action Plan

To be able to answer the research question, the researcher of this study planned and conducted the actions below:
1. Submitted letter of intent and research proposal to the principal for approval.
2. After the approval, the researcher divided the table tennis players into two groups. Group A had undergone multi-balls feeding 3 times a week

for two (2) weeks (July 7 – 18, 2014) before doing their usual routine (individual/dual match), and Group B had not.

    2.1. After two weeks of practice, the researcher gave them a 20 – Ball Feeding Post- Test on July 18, 2015 to check if there was improvement in their ability to receive balls correctly using the Backhand Topspin Stroke.

3. The performance of the group that had undergone Multi-Balls feeding (Group A) was compared to the group that had not (Group B).

    3.1. The data was analyzed and interpreted.

    3.2. Findings and conclusions were drawn based from the gathered data.

4. Further research and recommendation were given based on the results of the study.

5. Crafted the final draft of the study.

6. Presented the final crafted study to the authorities for approval.

7. Realization of the recommendations of the study.

ACTIVITIES	TIME FRAME	RESOURCES NEEDED	Persons Involved	Success Indicator/ Remarks
1. Submission of the letter of intent and research proposal to the Principal	July 4, 2014	Bondpaper	Principal Researcher	Completed
2. Conduct of the Intervention.	July 7 – 18, 2014	Racket, balls, table, score sheet	Table tennis players Researcher	Successful
3. Collection and Interpretation of Data	July 18 – 31, 2014	Band paper, laptop	Researcher	Completed
4. Gave recommendations based on the results of the study.	July 31, 2014	Band paper	Researcher	Completed
5. Final crafting of the Study.	August 1 – 22, 2014	Band paper, laptop, printer	Researcher, English Critic, Statistician	Completed
6. Presentation of the Final Crafted Study to the Authorities for approval.	August 25 to September 5, 2014	Band paper, printer	SDS PSDS EPS, MAPEH Principal Statistician Researcher	Completed
7. Realization of the Recommendations of the Study.	September 8, 2014 to end of the School Year 2014 – 2015.	Table tennis equipment and facilities.	Principal, Table tennis players, Researcher/Coach	To be accomplished

Collection, Presentation and Interpretation of Data

The data presented on the tables below was taken during the Pre-test and Post-test for the table tennis players' accuracy in receiving or returning balls using the Forehand and Backhand Topspin Strokes.

TABLE 1
FOREHAND AND BACKHAND – TOPSPIN STROKE
"20 – Ball Feeding PRE – TEST"

NAME OF PLAYERS	FOREHAND	BACKHAND
1. Casido, Mylen	14	13
2. Tayong, Ana Mae	13	17
3. Calidguid, Rhealyn	16	14
4. Andaya, Celmar Anne	13	12
5. Cadayona, Deve Joy	13	7
6. Baldoza, Evamae	16	14
7. Calidguid, Mira Fe	12	11
8. Andaya, Mc Alenn Joan	18	13
9.Villaseca, Nick Vincent	15	16
10. Manalo, John Mark	17	15
MEAN SCORE	14.7	13.2

The data of the table presented above shows the number of correct returns of the Table Tennis Players using the Forehand and Backhand – Topspin Strokes during the 20 – Ball Feeding Pre - Test. The mean score of their Forehand – Topspin Stroke is 14.7, and the mean score of their Backhand – Topspin Stroke is only 13.2. The results of the tests further show that most of the Table Tennis Players are weak in returning or receiving balls using the Backhand – Topspin Strokes.

TABLE 2
BACKHAND TOPSPIN STROKE
"20 – Ball Feeding POST – TEST"

GROUP A HAD UNDERGONE "MULTI-BALLS FEEDING"			GROUP B HAD NOT UNDERGONE "MULTI – BALLS FEEDING"		
NAME	BACKHAND TOPSPIN STROKE SCORES		NAME	BACKHAND TOPSPIN STROKE SCORES	
	PRE-TEST	POST-TEST		PRE-TEST	POST-TEST

1. Andaya, Celmar Anne	12	17	1. Tayong, Ana Mae	17	17
2. Cadayona, Deve Joy	7	18	2. Calidguid, Rhealyn	14	14
3. Baldoza, Evamae	14	20	3. Villaseca, Nick Vincent	16	13
4. Andaya, Mc Alenn Joan	14	19	4. Manalo, John Mark	15	12
5. Casido, Mylen	13	15	5. Calidguid, Mira Fe	14	12
MEAN SCORE	**12**	**17.8**	**MEAN SCORE**	**15.2**	**13.6**

Based on Table Number 2, the Mean Score of the Group which had undergone Multi – Balls Feeding (Group A) during Pre – Test is 12 and during Post – Test is 17.8. The Group's Score has increased up to 48.8 percent, and all of the members have enhanced their ability to receive balls correctly using the Backhand – Topspin Stroke. While the Mean Score of the Group which had not undergone Multi – Balls Feeding (Group B) during Pre – Test and Post Test are 15.2 and 13.6 respectively. The score of the group has decreased to 10.5 percent, and most of the members have leveled down their performance in receiving or returning balls correctly using the Backhand – Topspin Stroke. Thus, Multi – Balls Feeding is an effective way to harness the Table Tennis Players' Ability in receiving or returning balls correctly.

Results

Based on the findings presented on the tables above, Multi – Balls Feeding is an effective way in enhancing the Table Tennis Athletes' skills in receiving or returning balls correctly using the Backhand Topspin Stroke.

Recommendation

In light with the findings of this study, the following recommendations are presented below:

1. The Table Tennis Coach must introduce Multi – Balls Feeding to his athletes as part of their warming up routine during their training sessions.
2. Since Multi – Balls Feeding is effective in enhancing the receiving skills of the table tennis players, it is better to use at least 100 balls to be fed to each player in each stroke (Forehand & Backhand), for the more balls to feed the more the effectivity to enhance the players' accuracy in receiving or returning balls correctly.
3. Thus, Manjuyod National High School shall provide balls needed for the trainings.

Printed in Great Britain
by Amazon.co.uk, Ltd.,
Marston Gate.